LITERATURE AND CRITIC

Art Projects • Bulletin Boards • Plot Summaries
Skill Building Activities • Independent Thinking

Written by John and Patty Carratello
Illustrated by: Theresa Wright

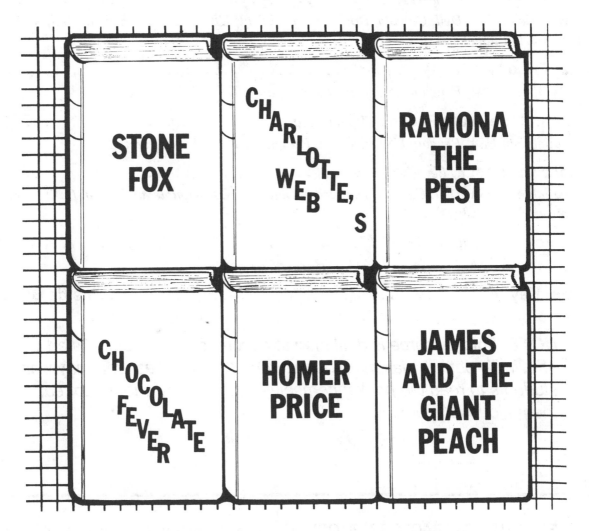

STONE FOX

CHARLOTTE'S WEB

RAMONA THE PEST

CHOCOLATE FEVER

HOMER PRICE

JAMES AND THE GIANT PEACH

Teacher Created Materials, Inc.
P.O. Box 1040
Huntington Beach, CA 92647
©*1987 Teacher Created Materials, Inc.*
Made in U.S.A.

ISBN 1-55734-355-1

Table of Contents

NOTE: *This resource is designed to accompany the books listed above. To obtain maximum benefit form the activities, you may want students to read the books themselves or you may choose to read them aloud to your class.*

FAVORITE CHARACTER MEMORY BOOK can be made by stapling together 12 sheets of paper. After each book unit, the children may select one character to receive the Favorite Character Award from page 20. They may color the award, fill in the information and paste the award in their award book.

On the opposite side of the paper, the children can draw and color a picture of their favorite character. A cover can be made to complete the book.

The Favorite Character Book will provide very enjoyable memories for the children in the future.

INTRODUCTION

LITERATURE FOR CRITICAL THINKING

It is possible for all children at varying developmental levels to engage in a discovery process which clarifies thinking, increases knowledge, and deepens their understanding of human issues and social values. This activities book, based on Bloom's *Taxonomy of Skills in the Cognitive Domain,* provides teachers a resource to maximize this process, using distinguished children's literature as a vehicle.

The authors suggest the following options in using this book:

OPTION 1:   The teacher may select a single activity for the entire class.

OPTION 2:   The teacher may select different activities for single students or small groups of students.

OPTION 3:   The student may select the level he or she wishes to work at, once the teacher explains what is available.

The stories in this book follow the same format, so that each level of thinking skills is approached as follows:

KNOWLEDGE

This level provides the child with an opportunity to recall fundamental facts and information about the story. Success at this level will be evidenced by the child's ability to:

Activity 1:   Match character names with pictures of the characters.

Activity 2:   Identify the main characters in a crossword puzzle.

Activity 3:   Match statements with the characters who said them.

Activity 4:   List the main characteristics of one of the main characters in a WANTED poster.

Activity 5:   Arrange scrambled story pictures in sequential order.

Activity 6:   Arrange scrambled story sentences in sequential order.

Activity 7:   Recall details about the setting by creating a picture of where a part of the story took place.

COMPREHENSION

This level provides the child with an opportunity to demonstrate a basic understanding of the story. Success at this level will be evidenced by the child's ability to:

Activity 1:   Interpret pictures of scenes from the story.

Activity 2:	Explain selected ideas or parts from the story in his or her own words.
Activity 3:	Draw a picture showing what happened before and after a passage or illustration found in the book.
Activity 4:	Write a sentence explaining what happened before and after a passage or illustration found in the book.
Activity 5:	Predict what *could* happen next in the story before the reading of the entire book is completed.
Activity 6:	Construct a pictorial time line which summarizes what happens in the story.
Activity 7:	Explain how the main character felt at the beginning, middle, and/or end of the story.

APPLICATION

This level provides the child with an opportunity to use information from the story in a new way. Success at this level will be evidenced by the child's ability to:

Activity 1:	Classify the characters as human, animal, or thing.
Activity 2:	Transfer a main character to a new setting.
Activity 3:	Make finger puppets and act out a part of the story.
Activity 4:	Select a meal that one of the main characters would enjoy eating, plan a menu, and a method of serving it.
Activity 5:	Think of a situation that occurred to a character in the story and write about how he or she would have handled the situation differently.
Activity 6:	Give examples of people the child knows who have the same problems as the characters in the story.

ANALYSIS

This level provides the child with an opportunity to take parts of the story and examine these parts carefully in order to better understand the whole story. Success at this level will be evidenced by the child's ability to:

Activity 1:	Identify general characteristics (stated and/or implied) of the main characters.
Activity 2:	Distinguish what could happen from what couldn't happen in the story in real life.
Activity 3:	Select parts of the story that were funniest, saddest, happiest, and most unbelievable.
Activity 4:	Differentiate fact from opinion.
Activity 5:	Compare and/or contrast two of the main characters.
Activity 6:	Select an action of a main character that was exactly the same as something the child would have done.

SYNTHESIS

This level provides the child with an opportunity to put parts from the story together in a new way to form a new idea or product. Success at this level will be evidenced by the child's ability to:

Activity 1: Create a story from just the title *before* the story is read (pre-story exercise).

Activity 2: Write three new titles for the story that would give a good idea what it was about.

Activity 3: Create a poster to advertise the story so people will want to read it.

Activity 4: Create a new product related to the story.

Activity 5: Restructure the roles of the main characters to create new outcomes in the story.

Activity 6: Compose and perform a dialogue or monologue that will communicate the thoughts of the main character(s) at a given point in the story.

Activity 7: Imagine that he or she is one of the main characters and write a diary account of daily thoughts and activities.

Activity 8: Create an original character and tell how the character would fit into the story.

Activity 9: Write the lyrics and music to a song that one of the main characters would sing if he/she/it became a rock star — and perform it.

EVALUATION

This level provides the child with an opportunity to form and present an opinion backed up by sound reasoning. Success at this level will be evidenced by the child's ability to:

Activity 1: Decide which character in the selection he or she would most like to spend a day with and why.

Activity 2: Judge whether or not a character should have acted in a particular way and why.

Activity 3: Decide if the story really could have happened and justify reasons for decision.

Activity 4: Consider how this story can help the child in his or her own life.

Activity 5: Appraise the value of the story.

Activity 6: Compare this story with another one the child has read.

Activity 7: Write a recommendation as to why the book should be read or not.

In addition to the activities just outlined, a class project and a small groups project will be included for each story.

CRITICAL THINKING
for
Charlotte's Web

by E.B. White

Mr. Arable has decided to kill the runt of a pig's litter. But his daughter Fern becomes so upset at this prospect that he decides to give her the runt to raise as a pet. She does, and names her new pet Wilbur. Later, when Wilbur is sold to Mr. Zuckerman, he learns from his barnyard friends that he will eventually be killed and used for food. He cries for help and is heard by a kindly spider named Charlotte. She spins words in her web to convince Mr. Zuckerman that Wilbur is a "terrific," very special pig. After several of Charlotte's words and a country fair prize, Zuckerman is convinced, and Wilbur's life is saved.

CHARLOTTE'S WEB
Story Pictures

Here are four pictures of things that happen in the story. Color each picture and cut it out. Decide which picture should come first, second, third, and fourth. Paste the pictures in order on a piece of 6" x 18" construction paper.

Wilbur meets Charlotte.

Wilbur wins a medal at the fair.

Fern raises a baby pig.

Charlotte weaves a word in her web.

7

Who would say a thing like that?

Cut out these word "bubbles." Match them with the characters who might say them. Paste the word bubbles over the blank bubbles next to the characters.

8

Who would say a thing like that?

Color the pictures. Paste the word bubbles in the blank bubbles next to the characters who *might* say them.

Main Events

These are pictures of Wilbur with friends who helped to keep him from being killed. Write a sentence that tells how each friend helped Wilbur.

Your sentence: _____

_____

_____

_____

Your sentence: _____

_____

_____

_____

10

In Your Words. . .

Read these ideas from the story. After you read each idea, explain what each idea means in your own words.

Doctor Dorian thinks that animals might talk more if people talked less.

_____

_____

_____

_____

_____

Charlotte thinks that she made her life better by helping Wilbur.

_____

_____

_____

_____

_____

Wilbur thinks that no one can ever take the place of Charlotte in his heart.

_____

_____

_____

_____

_____

Guess Who!

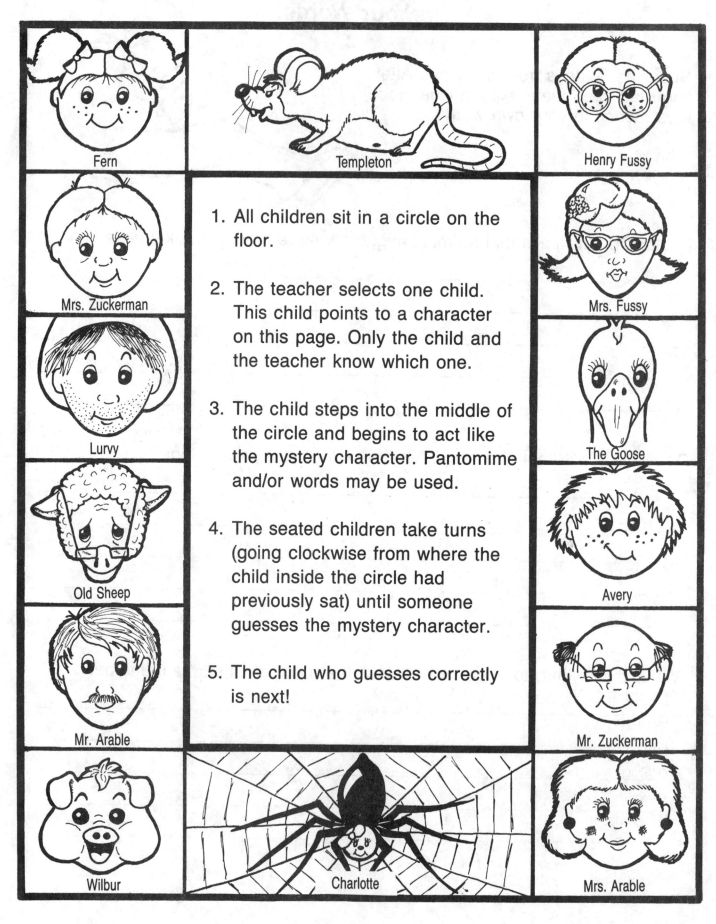

Fern

Templeton

Henry Fussy

Mrs. Zuckerman

Mrs. Fussy

Lurvy

The Goose

Old Sheep

Avery

Mr. Arable

Mr. Zuckerman

Wilbur

Charlotte

Mrs. Arable

1. All children sit in a circle on the floor.

2. The teacher selects one child. This child points to a character on this page. Only the child and the teacher know which one.

3. The child steps into the middle of the circle and begins to act like the mystery character. Pantomime and/or words may be used.

4. The seated children take turns (going clockwise from where the child inside the circle had previously sat) until someone guesses the mystery character.

5. The child who guesses correctly is next!

12

Visitor!

What would Wilbur be like if he came out of the book to visit you?

Answer these questions the way you think Wilbur would answer them.

1. Wilbur, what would it be like to have you live with me at my house? _____

   _____

   _____

2. Wilbur, what would it be like to have you walk to school with me? _____

   _____

   _____

3. Wilbur, what would it be like if you came to my classroom with me? _____

   _____

   _____

4. Wilbur, what would it be like if you played with my friends and me? _____

   _____

   _____

Make this Wilbur paper bag puppet.
When you have finished your Wilbur
puppet, use Wilbur to tell the class
one of your answers to the
questions above.

Wilbur Paper Bag Puppet

1. Color and cut out all pattern pieces.

2. With the bottom flap of a lunch bag facing up, glue the head to this flap.

3. Lift the bottom flap and glue the mouth under this flap.

4. Draw a body onto the lunch bag. Color.

5. Paste two legs, one on either side of the body, towards the top of Wilbur's body.

6. Paste two legs, one on either side of the body, at the bottom of Wilbur's body.

7. Turn the bag over. Paste the tail in the center about half way down on the bag.

14

Wilbur Paper Bag Puppet

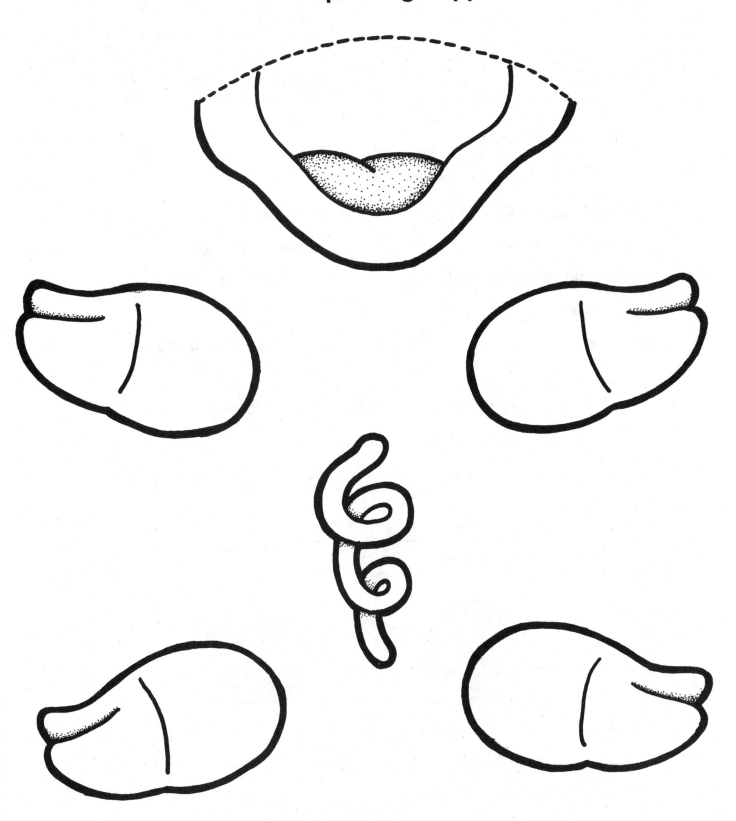

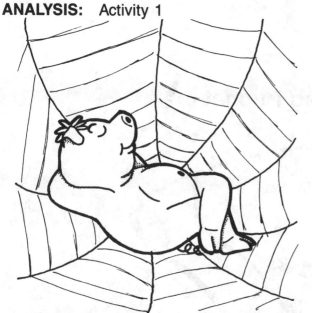

What could happen?

Some things in this story could happen in real life. Some things could not happen in real life. Read this list. Write the things from the list that could happen in Column 1. Write the things that could not happen in Column 2.

children ride a ferris wheel

pig spins a web

spider makes an egg sac

animals talk "people" talk

spider spins a web

spider spells words

goose sits on eggs

girl takes care of baby pig

rat reads words

spider sings to a pig

Column 1 — Things that could happen

1. _____

2. _____

3. _____

4. _____

5. _____

Column 2 — Things that could not happen

1. _____

2. _____

3. _____

4. _____

5. _____

Pick a part!

Select the parts of the story that you thought were the funniest, saddest, happiest, and most unbelievable.

The funniest part was _____

_____

_____

_____ .

The saddest part was _____

_____

_____ .

The happiest part was_____

_____

_____ .

The most unbelievable part was _____

_____

_____ .

Draw a picture of one of the parts you chose!

A New Creation!

What other word could Charlotte
have written about Wilbur?

1. Write a new word in the following box. Then, cut the box out and place
    your new word into the web you will trace over on page 19.

SOME PIG

RADIANT

TERRIFIC

HUMBLE

2. Put a spider in your web, too! Color this spider's body. Then, cut it out
    and place it somewhere on the web where you think it will look best.
    If you think you can, cut out the spider's legs. Otherwise, cut along the
    dotted line.

18

Charlotte's Web

I like . . .

Which one of the characters in the story do you like best? _____
Why? _____
_____

Which of the characters in the story do you like least?_____
Why? _____
_____

Make an award for your favorite character. Fill in the blanks on the ribbon.
Color the ribbon and cut it out. Put the ribbon in your **Favorite Characters**
memory book. (To be used with all story units — see table of contents
Favorite Character Memory Book, page 2.)

character's name →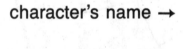

your name →

a few words about
your character →

book and author →

Because . . .

In *Charlotte's Web,* you learned the word *runt.* A runt is the smallest animal in a litter of baby animals born at the same time. You also learned that farmers, like Mr. Arable, often kill the runts that are born on a farm.

You will work in groups of four. Think together and answer these questions:

1. Why do you think Mr. Arable said, "A weakling makes trouble," when he talked to Fern about the new pig? _____

_____

_____

2. Read this part from the story:
"But it's unfair," cried Fern. "The pig couldn't help being born small, could it? If I had been very small at birth, would you have killed me?"

Mr. Arable smiled. "Certainly not," he said, looking down at his daughter with love. "But this is different. A little girl is one thing, a little runty pig is another."

"I see no difference," replied Fern, still hanging onto the ax. "This is the most terrible case of injustice I ever heard of."

Now, think of one reason why Mr. Arable might be right. _____

_____

Think of one reason why Fern may be right. _____

_____

Do you agree with Fern or Mr. Arable? _____
Why? _____

_____

3. Why do you think Mr. Arable finally let Fern keep Wilbur instead of killing him?_____

_____

_____

CHARLOTTE'S WEB SMALL GROUPS PROJECT

Save Our Friend!

Mr. Zuckerman doesn't believe the web any more. Wilbur is in danger! All Wilbur's friends want to put on a rock concert to save Wilbur. Each friend will sing a song at the "SAVE WILBUR" concert!

The teacher will assign you to work in groups of two, three or four.

1. Each group will select one of Wilbur's friends to write a song for.

2. Each group will then write a song for the "SAVE WILBUR" concert.

3. Each group (one or more of the members) will perform the song for the class. (If the group members like, they may make costumes and props to use for the performance. Examples of props would be guitars, drums or microphones.)

Write the words to your song here.

Title: _____

_____

_____

_____

_____

_____

_____

_____

_____

_____

_____

CHARLOTTE'S WEB CLASS PROJECT

Teacher's Directions

1. Cover a bulletin board with a light-colored background.

2. Mark the center points of each side and attach a piece of colored yarn (you may use string) from the center point of one side to the center point of the opposite side (A to B, C to D). Use staples (at the ends only) and make sure the yarn is pulled fairly tightly.

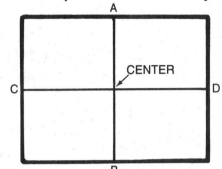

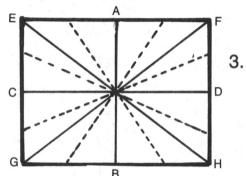

3. Begin to criss cross. First connect E to H and G to F (again, tightly). Then continue making "spokes" until you have evenly spaced spokes about 2 to 3 inches apart at the perimeter.

4. Cover the perimeter (so the staples don't show) with a border. You may want the border to look like wood from a barn.

5. Starting from the center of the board, begin to weave the rest of your web, making a tie attachment where you begin, and then going around clockwise (see picture). Alternate under and over each consecutive spoke. But don't pull too tightly. You may have to hold one weave while you pull the yarn over the next spoke, to hold the shape.

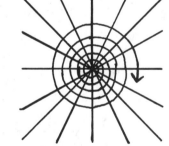

6. When you have reached the border, or when you feel you have enough web, tie off the yarn and cut off the excess.

7. Place a small drop of glue wherever yarn touches the spokes to secure the shape of the web.

8. Construct students' spiders and attach "feet" to the web with pins or staples. You may wish to hang some of the spiders from the ceiling so they hang in front of the web.

CHARLOTTE'S WEB CLASS PROJECT

Teacher's Directions, continued

OPTION: You may wish to construct a 3-dimensional web, using the same idea as before.

1. Find a space on the ceiling or in the corner of the room.

2. Find three or four connect points and string a continuous piece of yarn from point to point, attaching *very* securely at each point.

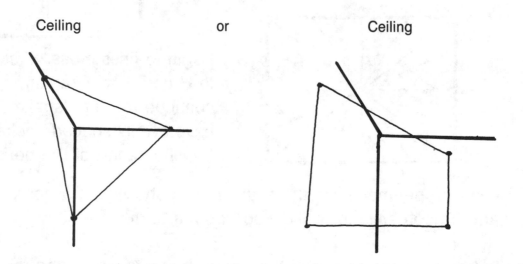

Ceiling   or   Ceiling

3. Use the same procedures as before, except tie your spokes to the perimeter made of yarn.

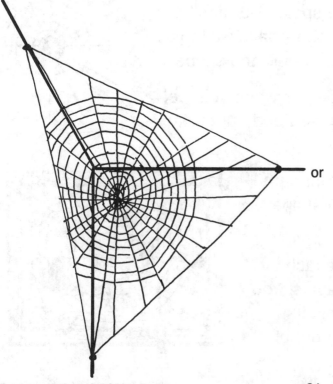 or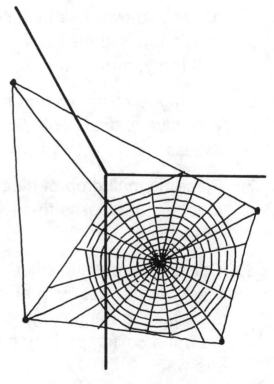

CHARLOTTE'S WEB CLASS PROJECT

Students' Directions

1. Think of a good word for Charlotte to spin in her web. Write it on the lines in the spider's body.

2. Write your name on the spider's body in a place you choose.

3. Color the spider's body and cut it out.

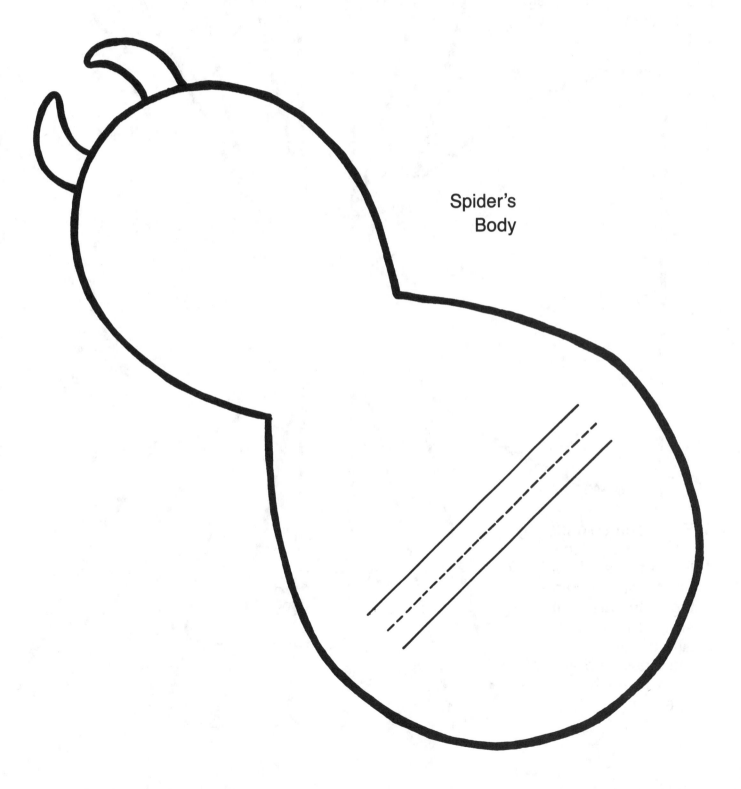

Spider's
Body

Students' Directions, continued

Spider's Legs

1. Read the fold up and fold down directions. Remember that the end broken line is folded up and the other broken line is folded down.
2. Color the spider's legs and cut them out carefully.

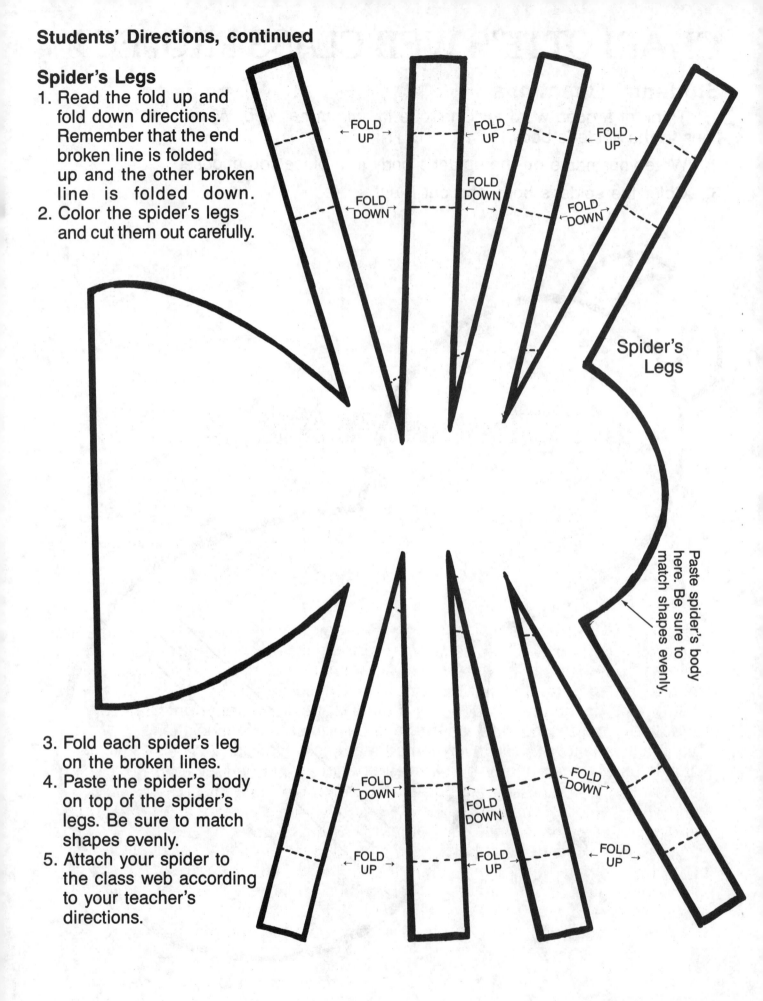

FOLD UP

FOLD UP

FOLD UP

FOLD DOWN

FOLD DOWN

FOLD DOWN

Spider's Legs

Paste spider's body here. Be sure to match shapes evenly.

FOLD DOWN

FOLD DOWN

FOLD DOWN

FOLD UP

FOLD UP

FOLD UP

3. Fold each spider's leg on the broken lines.
4. Paste the spider's body on top of the spider's legs. Be sure to match shapes evenly.
5. Attach your spider to the class web according to your teacher's directions.

Chocolate Fever

by Robert K. Smith

Henry Green loves chocolate. He loves it any way he can get it and eats as much of it as he can. Then one day, Henry breaks out with brown spots all over his body. The spots remain a mystery until a hospital lab report identifies them as being pure chocolate. Henry has "Chocolate Fever!"

But being poked and prodded as a medical freak isn't any fun. So Henry runs away from the hospital where he is being held for observation. Eventually, a kindly truck driver named Mac picks him up.

Later, as Mac gets ready to return Henry home, Henry, Mac, and the truck are hijacked for a supposed cargo of furs. Well, the "furs" turn out to be candy bars, and so, the befuddled hijackers take Henry, Mac, and the load of candy to their hideout until they can decide what to do.

Soon after arriving, neighborhood dogs, fresh on the scent of chocolate, break into the hideout, pounce upon the hijackers, and lick Henry all over! After the police take the hijackers away, Henry and Mac deliver the candy to Alfred Cane, a candy distributor who also had Chocolate Fever as a boy. Cane tells Henry what he must do to rid himself of his affliction!

Henry

Draw a picture of what Henry looks like with Chocolate Fever.

What Happens When?

Here are five sentences about things that happen in **Chocolate Fever.** Write them on the lines below in the order they happen in the story.

• Henry runs away from Dr. Fargo and the hospital.

• Louie and Lefty hijack Mac, Henry, and the truck.

• Henry Green feels strange, hears pops, and sees brown spots on his body.

• Boys in a schoolyard call Henry ugly.

• Alfred Cane gives Henry the cure for Chocolate Fever.

First: _____

_____

Second: _____

_____

Third: _____

_____

Fourth: _____

_____

Fifth: _____

_____

Hijacked!

Mac, Henry, and Mac's truck were hijacked by two robbers who thought the truck carried a cargo of furs. What **was** the cargo in Mac's truck?

_____

Disappointed with the robbery, the thieves took Mac and Henry to a secret hideout. Write what happened in the hideout that led to the capture of the thieves. Draw a picture of what happened too!

_____
_____
_____
_____
_____
_____
_____

PICTURE

The Cure!

Alfred Cane told Henry there was a two-part cure for Chocolate Fever.

The first part, and the harder part, was to learn this lesson:
"Although life is grand, and pleasure is everywhere, we can't have everything we want every time we want it!"

1. What did Alfred Cane mean by these words? _____

   _____

   _____

   _____

   _____

   _____

   _____

2. What was the second part of the cure?_____

   _____

   _____

   _____

3. Why would this part of the cure work? _____

   _____

   _____

   _____

   _____

   _____

A Chocolate Day!

Plan a "chocolate" day for Henry Green. What might he eat and drink for breakfast, lunch, snack, and dinner? **You** plan his menu! Write the food choices inside each plate and the drink choices under each glass.

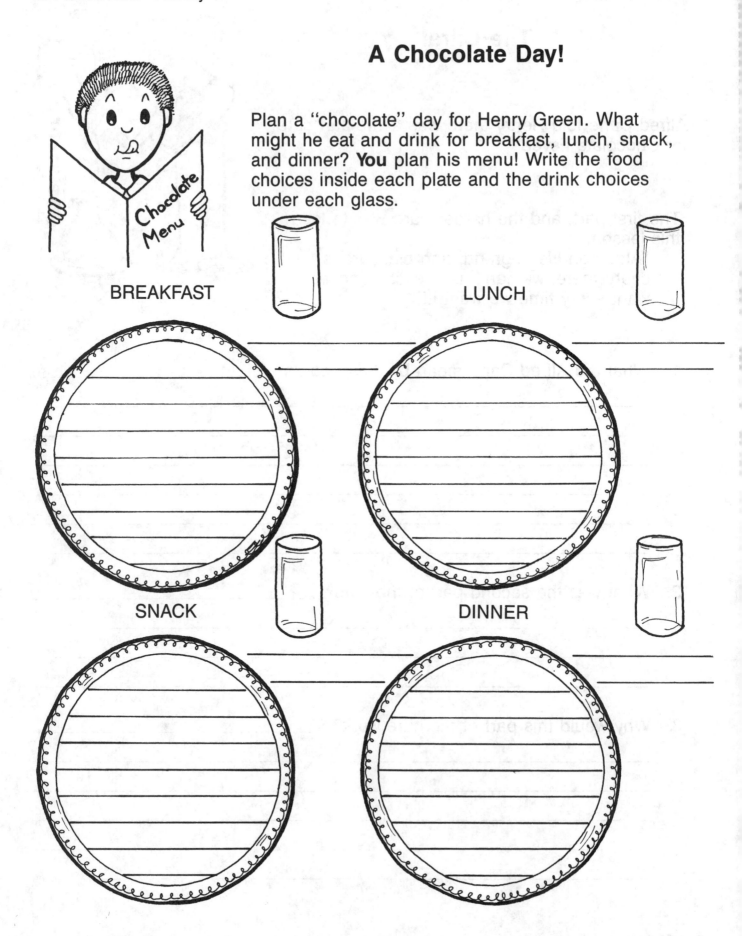

BREAKFAST

LUNCH

SNACK

DINNER

32

Who Else?

Henry loved chocolate more than any other food. Do people you know like one food more than any other food? _____ Do you? _____

Write the names of people you know who like one food so much they could eat it every day. Write the favorite food next to the person's name. Think of people who are your friends and in your family. Don't forget yourself!

NAME OF PERSON	FAVORITE FOOD
1. _____	1. _____
2. _____	2. _____
3. _____	3. _____
4. _____	4. _____
5. _____	5. _____
6. _____	6. _____
_____	_____

Parents!

Henry's Parents, Mr. and Mrs. Green, let him eat as much chocolate as he liked. In fact, they always kept chocolate things in the house for him.

1. Do you think **your** parents would let **you** eat as much chocolate as you would like?_____

   Why?_____

   _____

   _____

2. Do you think the parents of your friends would let them eat as much chocolate as they would like? _____

   Why?_____

   _____

   _____

3. Do you think Mr. and Mrs. Green should have let Henry eat so much chocolate? _____

   Why?_____

   _____

   _____

4. After Henry's Chocolate Fever was gone at the end of the story, Mrs. Green offered Henry his favorite chocolate syrup for his pancakes. Do you think this was a good thing for Mrs. Green to do? _____

   Why?_____

   _____

   _____

34

Stared At!

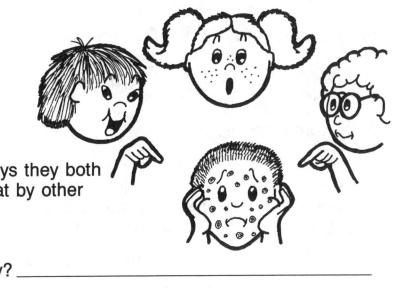

Henry and Mac are alike. Mac says they both know what it is like to be stared at by other people.

1. Why do people stare at Henry? _____
   _____
   _____
   _____

2. Why do people stare at Mac? _____
   _____
   _____
   _____

3. Do people stare at you? _____ Why? _____
   _____
   _____
   _____

4. Do you feel good when others stare at you? _____
   Why? _____
   _____
   _____

5. Do you stare at other people? _____
   Do you think it makes other people feel good when others stare at them?
   _____
   Why? _____
   _____
   _____

35

Class Favorites

My favorite food is: _____

_____

1. Draw and cut out small pictures of your **favorite** food, enough for each class member to have one.

2. Write your name on the front side of each food piece.

3. Exchange food pieces with your classmates.

4. Paste the class favorites on a paper plate that your teacher will give you. Be sure not to cover the other foods you have already pasted on. You may need more than one plate!

Here is an example of what your plate might look like.

A Poem About Chocolate

Work in groups of two or three.

1. Decide whether your group loves or hates chocolate. Then, write a group poem about your feelings for chocolate. You may want to write about how chocolate looks, smells, feels, and tastes. You might want to include how you feel when you eat it. You could add ways to prepare chocolate or ways to avoid eating it.

2. Write your poem in the shape below.

3. Draw a large picture of something chocolate. Make your picture large enough for the chocolate kiss below to be pasted inside.

4. Cut out the poem and paste it in your picture.

5. Make a class display of chocolate pictures and poems!

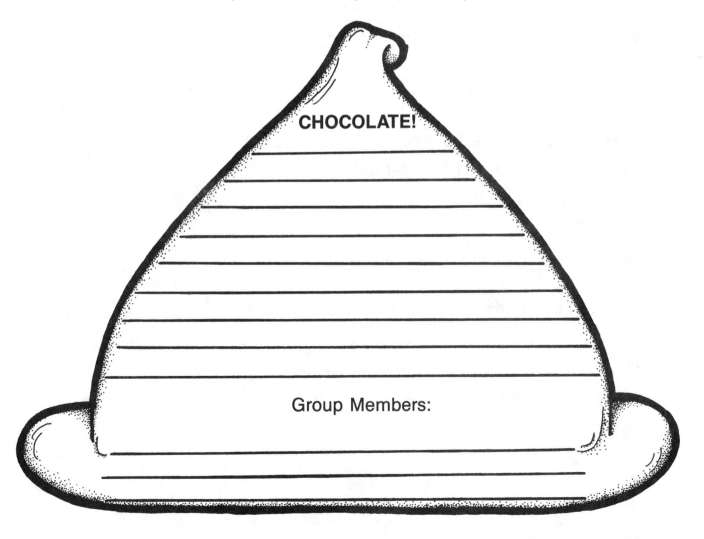

CHOCOLATE!

Group Members:

Cinnamon Fever!

At the beginning of the story, Henry eats too much chocolate. However, by the end of the story, he is not as interested in chocolate. He tries some cinnamon on his pancakes and starts thinking about all the things cinnamon would taste good on. He asks himself if there could be such a thing as "Cinnamon Fever."

1. What do you think? Could there be Cinnamon Fever? _____
   _____
   Why?_____
   _____
   _____
   _____

2. Should he have learned a lesson from chocolate? _____
   What lesson should he have learned? _____
   _____
   _____
   _____

3. What do you think Henry should do about using cinnamon? _____
   _____
   Why?_____
   _____
   _____
   _____

Don't Call Me Names!

The boys playing in the schoolyard called Henry ugly. They kept calling Henry names even though he tried to be polite. They were mean to him.

1. Would you have called Henry ugly if he was walking by you? _____

   Why?_____

   _____

   _____

2. Do you think people like to be called names? _____Why? _____

   _____

   _____

3. Have you ever called someone a name? _____Why? _____

   _____

   _____

4. How do you think that person might have felt?_____

   _____

   _____

5. Have you ever been called a name? _____

   If so, how did you feel? _____

   _____

   _____

   _____

Homer Price

by Robert McCloskey

Homer Price is a smart, responsible boy who has six adventures to be told. He captures four robbers with the help of his pet skunk Aroma, and comes to the aid of a Superhero. In other adventures, he makes and devises a way to sell hundreds of doughnuts, and helps his uncle win the girl of his dreams. Homer prevents a pied-piper-type calamity from occuring to the town. He is also there to help when a new part of town is built.

Homer Price is the local hero!

Put Me In My Place, Please!

Write the name of each character or thing in the word box under the correct story on the lines below.

Naomi Enders	houses	Super-Duper
a suitcase	Michael Murphy	Yarn
Miss Terwilliger	Mr. Gabby	Aroma
music	comic books	Robbers
Dulcey Dooner	Uncle Telemachus	Freddy
doughnut machine	mice	bracelet

1. "The Case of the Sensational Scent"
   1) _____ 2) _____
   3) _____

2. "The Case of the Cosmic Comic"
   1) _____ 2) _____
   3) _____

3. "The Doughnuts"
   1) _____ 2) _____
   3) _____

4. "Mystery Yarn"
   1) _____ 2) _____
   3) _____

5. "Nothing New Under The Sun (Hardly)"
   1) _____ 2) _____
   3) _____

6. "Wheels Of Progress"
   1) _____ 2) _____
   3) _____

Who Was That Stranger?

In the story "Nothing New Under The Sun (Hardly)," there was a stranger who made the people of Centerburg *very* curious. The whole town wondered who he was.

"Who was this stranger? Where did he come from? Where was he going? How long was his beard and his hair? What was his name? Did he have a business? What could be on the back of his car that was so carefully covered with the large canvas?"

How many of the town's questions can you answer?

1. Who was this stranger? _____

    _____

2. Where did he come from? _____

    _____

3. Where was he going? _____

    _____

4. How long was his beard and his hair? _____

    _____

5. What was his name? _____

6. Did he have a business? _____

    _____

7. What could be on the back of his car that was so carefully covered with the large canvas? _____

    _____

42

Homer Price In Our Class!

Create a **Homer Price** mural for bulletin board in the classroom.

Teacher:

1. Divide the class into six groups.

2. Assign each group a story from **Homer Price.**
   "The Case of the Sensational Scent"
   "The Case of the Cosmic Comic"
   "The Doughnuts"
   "Mystery Yarn"
   "Nothing New Under The Sun (Hardly)"
   "Wheels Of Progress"

3. Give each group two weeks to complete a mural and a summary paragraph (to be affixed to the mural) explaining what happened in their assigned story.

4. Explain that each group member will assist the group in mural and paragraph planning. Then, tasks may be assigned for each member such as paragraph writing, drawing, constructing models, collecting yarn, coloring, painting, or anything else that may make the mural interesting.

Can You Guess?

Step 1.
Select a character from **Homer Price.**

_____

character's name

Step 2

Fill in the following sentence clues about your chosen character.

Clue #1: If I were to tell you how my character looks, I would say that _____

_____.

Clue #2: Something my character did was _____

_____.

Clue #3: Something my character said was, _____

_____.

Clue #4: I think/don't think (circle one) the story could have happened without
my character because _____

_____.

Step 3

Read your clues to the class one clue at a time. At the end of each clue, see
if anyone can guess your character. If no one can guess by the last clue, you
may tell the class the name of your character!

What Would Homer Do?

You and Homer are friends. Today you and Homer will do three things together. With him, Homer has Aroma the Skunk, paper, a pen, and about six feet of strong string he has been saving for Uncle Telly.

1. You and Homer are climbing rocks. Suddenly, you slip and fall off a large rock. Your foot catches on a rock ledge and you stop falling, but you can't climb back up. What would Homer do? _____

   _____

   _____

   _____

2. Homer has just helped you bake 1000 cookies for the school carnival. But, you can't find your watch. It must be in one of the cookies! What would Homer do? _____

   _____

   _____

   _____

3. You and Homer are at the zoo watching the zookeeper feed the elephants. Suddenly, a woman screams, "Stop those two men. They took the zoo's money!" What would Homer do? _____

   _____

   _____

   _____

What Would You Do?

Homer Price has a few problems in it. Can you solve the problems below in a different way than you read about?

1. What would you do to stop the doughnut machine?_____
_____
_____

2. What would you do to get rid of all the mice in a town? _____
_____
_____
_____

3. What would you do to identify 100 homes without street signs? _____
_____
_____

46

ANALYSIS: Activity 1

I Can, Too!

Here are some things Homer Price did in the book:

1. Walked four robbers two miles with a skunk.
2. Made thousands of doughnuts.
3. Helped his parents take care of their tourist camp.
4. Read comic books with a friend.
5. Acted the part of an Indian in a play.
6. Found out things about a stranger.
7. Read about what music can do to people and animals.
8. Thought of a way to sell thousands of doughnuts.
9. Called the Sheriff for help.
10. Helped his Uncle Telly wind string.

What things from this list could you do, too? Write the sentence numbers

here: _____

_____

Think of three more things that Homer Price did in the story that you could

do, too.

1. _____

_____

2. _____

_____

3. _____

_____

Pick A Part!

1. What part of **Homer Price** was the funniest?_____
    _____
    _____

2. What part of **Homer Price** was the silliest?   _____
    _____
    _____

3. What part of **Homer Price** was the most believable?_____
    _____
    _____

4. What part of **Homer Price** was the most unbelievable? _____
    _____

5. When did Homer do the smartest thing? _____
    _____

6. When did Homer do the bravest thing?_____
    _____

7. When did Homer do something just like you would have done? _____
    _____
    _____

48

Homer Price?

What can you tell about a book from a title?

Before you read **Homer Price**, answer these questions.

1. What or who is Homer Price? (boy, girl, man, woman, animal, insect, monster, shopping store, or ?)

   I think Homer Price is _____

   _____

2. How old is Homer Price? _____

3. What does Homer Price look like? _____

   _____

   _____

4. What is one thing that Homer Price might do in the story? _____

   _____

   _____

   Draw a picture of Homer Price.

   [   ]

Sheriff!

The Sheriff in **Homer Price** does not always do the best job of being sheriff. He likes to sit in the barber shop and talk, sometimes for a *long* time.

How would "The Case of the Sensational Scent" be different if the town of Centerburg had a fast-acting sheriff?

_____

_____

_____

_____

_____

_____

_____

_____

_____

_____

_____

50

Superhero!

Before reading "The Case of the Cosmic Comic" answer these questions?

1. What is a Superhero? _____

   _____

   _____

2. Do you have a favorite Superhero? _____
   Who? _____

   _____

   _____

   _____

3. Is your Superhero real or pretend?_____
   Why?_____

   _____

After reading "The Case of the Cosmic Comic" answer these questions:

1. Who is Freddy's Superhero? _____

2. Is he real to Freddy? _____ How do you know?

   _____

3. Is he real to Homer Price? _____ How do you know?

   _____

4. Is he real to Freddy at the end of the story? _____
   How do you know? _____

   _____

5. Can believing in a Superhero be fun? _____
   How?

   _____

   _____

6. Can believing in a Superhero be dangerous? _____
   How?_____

   _____

My Reasons

Write one reason you liked or
did not like each of the
stories in **Homer Price.**

1. "The Case of the Sensational Scent" _____
   _____
   _____

2. "The Case of the Cosmic Comic" _____
   _____
   _____

3. "The Doughnuts" _____
   _____
   _____

4. "Mystery Yarn" _____
   _____
   _____

5. "Nothing New Under The Sun (Hardly)" _____
   _____
   _____

6. "Wheels of Progress" _____
   _____
   _____

Which one of these stories did you like the most? _____
_____

Why?_____
_____
_____

James
and the
Giant Peach
by Roald Dahl

James led a happy life until his parents were eaten by a rhinoceros and he had to live with his two selfish aunts. He was miserable until the day he got a bag of magic from a stranger. But on his way to the house, he dropped the bag under the withered peach tree near the top of the hill. The magic worked on the tree, producing an enormous peach. His aunts were very happy, charging money for people to see the giant peach. But they were still cruel to James. One evening, a tired and sad James found a hole in the peach. He entered the peach to find enormous (but friendly) bugs who had been changed by the magic, too!

When the peach stem is chewed by one of the bugs — causing the peach to roll over the aunts and down the hill — James and his new friends embark on a grand adventure aboard the giant peach.

WANTED!

Make a wanted poster for one of the characters in **James and the Giant Peach.** Here are some characters you might choose:

James	Centipede	Glow-worm
Aunt Sponge	Earthworm	Silkworm
Aunt Spiker	Miss Spider	Cloud-Men
Old Man	Ladybug	The Peach
Old-Green-Grasshopper		

Which one will you choose?_____

_____

DIRECTIONS:

1. Use the WANTED POSTER blank on the following page.
2. Draw a picture of your character in the rectangle.
3. Write the character's name under the picture.
4. List things that will help identify your character by filling in the blanks on the poster. Practice below, then after your teacher checks it, recopy the information neatly onto the WANTED POSTER.

Wanted for: (What is your character wanted for?)_____

_____

_____

Looks: (What does your character look like?) _____

_____

_____

Last seen: (When and where was your character last seen?) _____

_____

_____

Reward: (What is the reward for finding the character?) _____

_____

_____

WANTED!

Name: _____

Wanted for: _____

_____

_____

Looks: _____

_____

_____

Last seen: _____

_____

_____

Reward: _____

_____

_____

Who said that? (Bubbles)

Cut out these word "bubbles." Match them with the characters who said them. Paste the word bubbles over the blank bubbles next to the characters on the next page.

56

Who said that? (Characters)

Color the pictures. Paste the word bubbles in the blank bubbles next to the characters who said them.

Miss Spider

Old Man

Centipede

Aunt Sponge

James

Picture This!

Here are two pictures of things that happen in **James and the Giant Peach.**
Write a sentence to tell what is happening in each picture.

Picture 1: _____

_____

_____

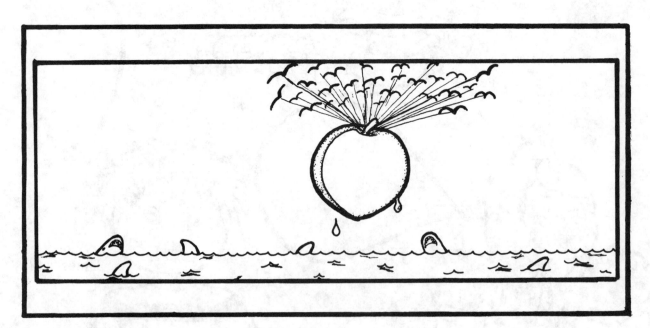

Picture 2: _____

_____

_____

How does James feel?

Answer these questions in complete sentences.

1. How does James feel when he lives with his parents by the sea?

   _____

   _____

   _____

2. How does James feel when he lives with his aunts on the hill?

   _____

   _____

   _____

3. How does James feel when he lives with the bugs in the peach?

   _____

   _____

   _____

4. How does James feel when he lives in the peach pit in the park?

   _____

   _____

   _____

On the back of this paper, draw a picture of James in one of these places.

What is it?

What are these characters? Are they people or animals? Are they bugs or make-believe creatures? Write the name of each character in its group on the lines below.

Centipede	James Henry
Aunt Sponge	Trotter
Miss Spider	Cloud-Men
Sharks	Ladybug
Seagulls	Glow-Worm
Earthworm	Old Man
Old-Green-	The Mayor
Grasshopper	Rhinoceros
Silkworm	Aunt Spiker

PEOPLE

1. _____

2. _____

3. _____

4. _____

5. _____

BUGS

1. _____

2. _____

3. _____

4. _____

5. _____

6. _____

7. _____

ANIMALS

1. _____

2. _____

3. _____

MAKE-BELIEVE CREATURES

1. _____

60

Meal Time!

In Chapter 18, the Centipede sings a song about all the food he likes to eat. Read the song again.

Use ideas from the song or ideas of your own to plan a meal for the Centipede. Answer the questions below. Then, create your meal for the Centipede. Use yarn, macaroni, cereal, dried weeds, colored paper, crayons, rice, or other materials to make your "meal." (Please, no squashed bugs or other living or once living creatures.)

Paste your meal on a paper plate and tell your classmates about it!

1. What would the meal for the Centipede be? _____

_____

_____

2. How would you make the food? _____

_____

_____

3. How would you serve it to the Centipede? _____

_____

_____

What couldn't happen?

Some things in this story could not happen in real life. Some things could happen in real life. Read this list of things that happened in **James and the Giant Peach.** Color the giant peach in the box next to each thing that *could not* happen in real life. (Be ready to tell *why* they could not happen, too!)

1. A grasshopper makes musical sounds by rubbing his wings on his legs.

2. A rhinoceros eats two people on a crowded city street in 35 seconds.

3. A centipede always wears 42 boots before going out.

4. A peach grows as big as a small house.

5. Soil passes through the body of an earthworm, in one end and out the other.

6. Some insects do not have ears in their heads.

7. Weather changes are made by Cloud-Men, making snowballs, pouring buckets of water, and painting rainbows.

8. 502 seagulls carry a giant peach across the Atlantic Ocean.

9. Seven large bugs and a little boy live inside a peach pit.

10. James tells stories to children in a park in New York City.

My Story

You are about to read a story called **James and the Giant Peach.** What do you think the story will be about?

Write your ideas for a story here. Tell as much of a story as you can from just knowing the title. Have fun!

**JAMES AND THE GIANT PEACH
MY STORY**

_____

_____

_____

_____

_____

_____

_____

_____

_____

_____

_____

What If...?

What if James had not dropped the bag of green things under the peach tree? What if he had swallowed them all instead? How would the story be different?

_____

_____

_____

_____

_____

_____

Write five marvelous, fabulous, unbelievable things that might have happened to James if he had eaten the green things.

1. _____

_____

2. _____

_____

3. _____

_____

4. _____

_____

5. _____

_____

On the back of this paper, draw one of the things you wrote about. Share your ideas with the class!

The Perfect Life

Until James Henry Trotter was four, he lived the perfect life for a boy, or so he thought.

What is your idea of a perfect life? Write about what would be the perfect life for you.

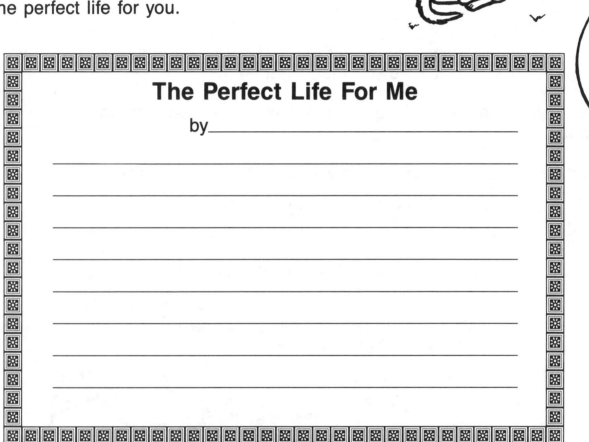

The Perfect Life For Me

by_____

_____

_____

_____

_____

_____

_____

_____

_____

_____

Cut this out and paste it on a large piece of construction paper. On the rest of the construction paper draw ideas of your perfect life or cut and paste pictures of your ideas from magazines.

Add your "perfect life" paper to a class bulletin board of all the perfect life ideas in your class. Read each other's ideas!

(Teacher: Make a "PERFECT LIFE" bulletin board heading.)

Teacher Option: Students may do art project if writing assignment is too difficult.

Bugs!

How much do you know about bugs? Many things Roald Dahl wrote about bugs in this story are true. These are the bugs in **James and the Giant Peach:**

centipede	silkworm	glow-worm
earthworm	grasshopper	ladybug
spider		

You will do a group project to find out more about these bugs and report your information to the class before you read Chapter 12.

There will be seven groups, one group for each bug. Each group will do the following:

1. Research chosen bug in encyclopedias and science books.

2. Write a short paper of information about the bug.

3. Make a picture or model of the bug.

4. Present the information to the class before reading Chapter 12.

Teacher: Help students establish responsibilities for each group member, such as: leader, writer, artist, researcher, presenter.

A Day With . . .

1. With which character in **James and the Giant Peach** would you most like to spend the day? _____

   Why?_____

   _____

   _____

   _____

   _____

2. What would you both do first? _____

   _____

   _____

3. Would you go to school together? _____ If so, describe your time at school._____

   _____

   _____

4. What would you both eat for meals and snacks?_____

   _____

   _____

5. What games could you play together? _____

   _____

   _____

6. What is one thing you could do with your character that you couldn't do with anybody else? _____

   _____

   _____

7. Would your character spend the night? _____ If so, how would you both sleep? _____

   _____

You Be The Judge!

1. Do you think Aunt Sponge and Aunt Spiker were right when they said that James was lazy and good-for-nothing? _____
Why?_____
_____
_____
_____
_____
_____

   Why do you think his aunts didn't like him? _____
_____
_____

2. Would you swallow little green things if a stranger told you that if you did, your life would be better?_____Why?_____
_____
_____

3. Would you like it if suddenly insects and spiders were as big as children?
_____ Why? _____
_____
_____

4. Why do you think the Centipede called the Cloud-Men names? _____
_____

5. Do you or people that you know call other people names? _____
Why?_____
_____
_____
_____

Ramona The Pest

by Beverly Cleary

    Ramona Quimby is five years old and has the reputation of being a bit of a pest. She is eagerly awaiting her first day at kindergarten but, once at school, finds that kindergarten is not exactly what she expected it to be. Ramona quickly finds herself the center of numerous mishaps. At one point, unable to resist "boinging" a little girl's springy curls, Ramona is sent home by her teacher, Miss Binney, until her behavior improves. Ramona, the kindergarten dropout, stays home sadly, fearing that she has lost her beloved teacher's affection. But Miss Binney sends her a note, along with Ramona's first tooth that had come out in class. In the note, Miss Binney asks Ramona when she will return. "Loved" once again by her teacher, Ramona eagerly readies herself to return!

Match These!

Match these characters with their descriptions

_____	1. Beezus	a.	helps the kindergarten children cross the street
_____	2. Susan	b.	understands children and is young and pretty
_____	3. Henry Huggins	c.	has green hair and was named after an aunt's car
_____	4. Miss Binney	d.	wears reddish-brown, boing, boing curls
_____	5. Ramona	e.	shares a room with Ramona
_____	6. Howie	f.	is loved and chased by Ramona
_____	7. Mrs. Quimby	g.	is so sloppy she is interesting
_____	8. Willa Jean	h.	doesn't get excited about things and is great with tools
_____	9. Davy	i.	makes big, noisy fusses
_____	10. Chevrolet	j.	is a slow-poke grown up who makes a witch's costume

Who Said That?

Write the name of each character on the
line next to what the character said. Use the
names in the Wordbox to help you.

Ramona   Susan   Mrs. Quimby

Miss Binney   Henry Huggins   Howie

1. "I am sorry I forgot to give you your tooth, but I am sure the tooth fairy
   will understand. When are you coming back to kindergarten?"

   1._____

2. "You stop boinging me!"

   2._____

3. "Miss Binney is not going to forget you . . . Not ever, as long as she lives."

   3._____

4. "I am **not** a pest."

   4._____

5. "I like to take wheels off tricycles."

   5._____

6. "Do you want us both to land in the mud?"

   6._____

New Boots!

1. Color Ramona's new boots the right color.

2. Explain how Ramona felt about her new boots. _____

   _____

   _____

   _____

3. Draw a picture of what happened to Ramona and her new boots on the first day she wore them to school.

In Your Words...

Explain why Ramona did these things:

1. Stayed so long in her seat on the first day of kindergarten.

   _____

   _____

   _____

2. Pulled Susan's hair.

   _____

   _____

   _____

3. Chased Davy.

   _____

   _____

   _____

4. Snored during nap time.

   _____

   _____

   _____

5. Held her name on her witch's costume in the Halloween parade.

   _____

   _____

   _____

6. Hid behind the trash cans instead of going to class.

   _____

   _____

   _____

7. Did not want to go back to kindergarten.

   _____

   _____

   _____

Class Pests!

Things we do can sometimes bother other people. Can you think of something that **you** do that might bother someone else? It could be someone at home, in your neighborhood, or at school.

This is a PEST POSTER! Fill it in, cut it out, and put it on a class bulletin board called CLASS PESTS!

_____ ← Write your first name here.

the Pest!

Draw or paste your picture here.

_____ is a pest because ← Write your first name.
                                                  ← Write the pesty thing you do.
_____
_____
_____

This pesty thing bothers

_____ ← Write who this pesty thing bothers.

very much!

She's Here!

Ramona is not in kindergarten any more. She just became a student in **YOUR** class. What will she do now that she's in your class?

Work in groups of two or three. In your groups, think of five things Ramona might do in your class. Write them on this page. Under each thing she does, write her reason for doing it!

1. _____

_____

Reason: _____

_____

2. _____

_____

Reason: _____

_____

3. _____

_____

Reason: _____

_____

4. _____

_____

Reason: _____

_____

5. _____

_____

Reason: _____

_____

ANALYSIS: Activity 1

Ramona And Me!

Have you ever splashed in the rain and jumped in mud? Have you ever pulled someone's hair? Have you ever been frightened by a Halloween mask?

These are just some of the things that happened to Ramona. Choose **one** of the many things that Ramona did that you have done or would do!

Write it here:_____

_____

_____

_____

Draw a picture of you doing it!

Is Ramona A Pest?

Would you call Ramona a pest? _____

Why? _____

_____

_____

_____

What do you think a pest is? _____

_____

_____

_____

Look up "pest" in the dictionary. Write the definition here. _____

_____

Do you think Ramona is a pest the way pest is explained in the dictionary?

_____ Why? _____

_____

Ramona did not think she was a pest, but other people believed she was. What are some things Ramona did to make other people call her a pest?

1. _____

_____

2. _____

_____

3. _____

_____

Choose one of the "pesty" things you wrote that Ramona did. Explain why Ramona did it. Try to convince us that it was not a "pesty" thing to do.

_____

_____

_____

My Initial!

What animal did Ramona make out of the first letter of her last name?

_____

Make a picture out of the first letter of **your** last name inside this box. Cut the box out. Put your letter picture on a class bulletin board.

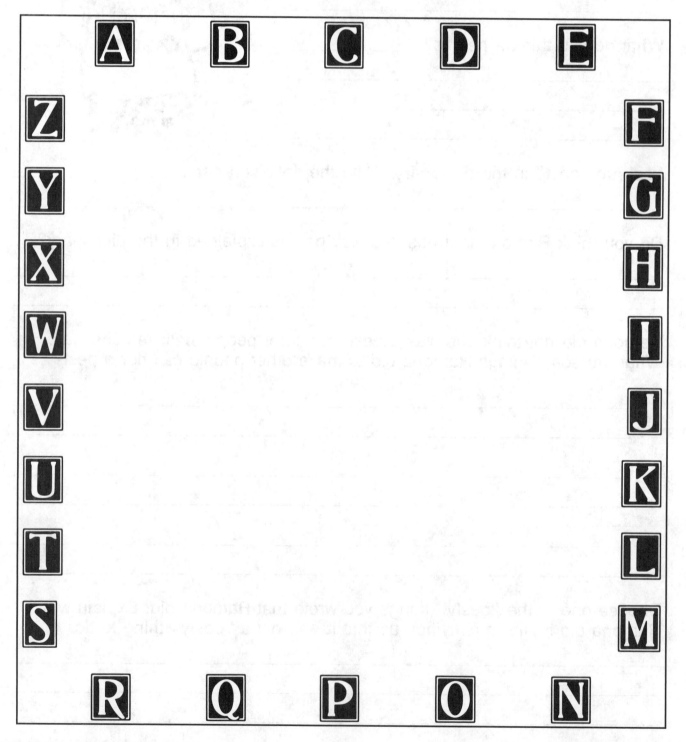

Dear Diary

Pretend **you** are Ramona and have a diary. Write a diary entry of three things that could happen during a day as Ramona.

Date_____

Dear Diary,

This morning I got up, dressed for school in these clothes: _____

_____,

and ate _____for breakfast.

On my way to school _____

_____

_____

_____

_____

_____

During class_____

_____

_____

_____

_____

At lunchtime_____

_____

_____

_____

_____

These are just some of the things that happened to me today!

EVALUATION: Activity 1

Remember When?

Did you like **your** first day at kindergarten?
_____Why?_____

_____

_____

_____

_____

How did **you** feel about being in school?_____

_____

_____

What was your teacher's name? _____

What is one thing you remember about your teacher?_____

_____

_____

What is one thing that you really liked about kindergarten? _____
Why?_____

_____

_____

_____

What is one thing that happened in kindergarten that you remember? _____

_____

_____

Would you have liked someone to read **Ramona the Pest** to you before you
started kindergarten? _____
Why?_____

_____

_____

Was Ramona Right?

Listed below are several situations Ramona got herself into. If you agree that Ramona did the right thing, write why you think she did it next to each situation. If you think Ramona should have acted differently, write what you think she should have done next to each situation.

"BOING"

1. Ramona pulled Susan's hair. _____

_____

_____

_____

2. Ramona hid behind trash cans instead of going to kindergarten the day the substitute was there. _____

_____

_____

_____

3. Ramona snored during nap time. _____

_____

_____

_____

4. Ramona wore a worm on her finger. _____

_____

_____

_____

Stone Fox

by John R. Gardiner

   Little Willy lives with his grandfather on a potato farm in Wyoming. His grandfather has kept a secret from little Willy—ten years of unpaid back taxes equaling $500. Grandfather loses his will to live because of his fear that the farm will be lost to the unpaid taxes. But little Willy shoulders the responsibility of caring for his grandfather and the farm, and devises a way to make the money to pay the taxes. Little Willy enters the National Dogsled Race for a prize purse of $500, and is set to win with his faithful dog, Searchlight, pulling the sled. But little Willy encounters a formidable opponent in Stone Fox, the Shoshone Indian who has never lost a race. During the ten mile race, little Willy leads until 100 feet from the finish line, when Searchlight has a heart attack and dies. Touched by the boy and dog's will to win, Stone Fox keeps the other race contestants from the finish line as little Willy carries Searchlight over to win the race.

Crossword Puzzle

Complete the "across" and "down" sentences on the next page to do this crossword puzzle. Use the Wordbox to help you.

Crossword Puzzle Wordbox

"Across" Answers

win	Lester	Wyoming	five
Samoyeds	Main	years	Smith
yes	line	Searchlight	heart
Stone Fox	road	Dogsled	no

"Down" Answers

Snyder	Mayor	lake	potato
one	college	Shoshone	Willy
hundred	Foster	miles	taxes
Grandfather	eye		

Crossword Puzzle, continued

Across

1. Little Willy carried Searchlight across the finish __ __ __ __.
2. Little Willy's dog was __ __ __ __ __ __ __ __ __ __ __.
6. Little Willy and Stone Fox wanted to __ __ __ the race.
7. The dogsled race started on __ __ __ __ Street.
8. The dogs Stone Fox had were called __ __ __ __ __ __ __ __.
9. Little Willy and Searchlight were over ten __ __ __ __ __ old.
10. Searchlight had a __ __ __ __ __ attack and died.
13. When Grandfather put his hand palm up, it meant __ __ __.
15. The North __ __ __ __ was curvy, the South __ __ __ __ was straight.
16. __ __ __ __ __ __ __ __ was a Shoshone Indian.
18. When Grandfather put his hand palm down, it meant __ __.
21. The race was called the National __ __ __ __ __ __ __ Race.
22. Doc __ __ __ __ __ helped little Willy and Grandfather.
24. Stone Fox raced with __ __ __ __ Samoyeds.
25. __ __ __ __ __ __ at the General Store gave the race poster to little Willy.
26. The story took place in the state of __ __ __ __ __ __ __.

Down

1. Little Willy took a shortcut in the race across the frozen __ __ __ __.
2. Clifford __ __ __ __ __ __ was the tax collector.
3. The prize for the race winner was five __ __ __ __ __ __ __ dollars.
4. __ __ __ __ __ __ __ __ __ __ __ __ and little Willy lived together.
5. How many dogs did little Willy race with? __ __ __
6. Little __ __ __ __ __ tried to be friendly with Stone Fox.
7. __ __ __ __ __ Smiley collected the money for the race entry.
11. Stone Fox struck little Willy in the __ __ __ when little Willy came near his dogs.
12. Grandfather hadn't paid his back __ __ __ __ __.
14. Stone Fox was an Indian from the __ __ __ __ __ __ __ __ tribe.
17. Mr. __ __ __ __ __ __ was the banker.
19. Grandfather and little Willy had a __ __ __ __ __ __ farm.
20. Little Willy's bank money was supposed to be for a __ __ __ __ __ __ __ education.
23. The dogsled race was ten __ __ __ __ __.

Who Said What To Whom?

There are five quotations from **Stone Fox** on this page. Do you know who said each one? Do you know to whom the words were spoken?

Use the names in the word box to help you. A name may be used more than once.

---

little Willy • Mr. Foster • Searchlight

Doc Smith • Stone Fox • Clifford Snyder

• dogsled racers •

---

1. "I'm sorry, child, but it appears that your grandfather just doesn't want to live anymore."

_____ said this to _____.

2. "Anyone crosses this line—I shoot."

_____ said this to _____.

3. "You did real good, girl. Real good. I'm real proud of you. You rest now. Just rest."

_____ said this to _____.

4. "...the money in your savings account is for your college education. You know I can't give it to you."

_____ said this to _____.

5. "Every year we send a letter—a tax bill—showing how much you owe."

_____ said this to _____.

Grandfather says...

Little Willy's Grandfather taught him many things. He said things to little Willy that helped him learn about life.

What did Grandfather mean when he said these things to little Willy?

1. "It's good to ask questions."

_____

_____

_____

_____

_____

2. "Don't accept help unless you can pay for it, especially from friends."

_____

_____

_____

_____

_____

3. "Where there's a will, there's a way."

_____

_____

_____

_____

_____

What Will Happen?

You have just finished reading Chapter 9. Little Willy and Stone Fox are very close together in the dogsled race.

How do you think the race will end? Write a paragraph and draw a picture explaining what **you** think will happen in the race.

PARAGRAPH

_____

_____

_____

_____

_____

_____

PICTURE:

Money!

Little Willy entered a dogsled race to win the money to pay back taxes on his grandfather's farm.

How would **you** raise $500 if you were in the same situation as little Willy? Think of all the ways you could earn $500 and write them here. Remember, these have to be ways that you **really** could earn the money, not make-believe ways!

1. _____

_____

2. _____

_____

3. _____

_____

4. _____

_____

5. _____

_____

Share your ideas with the class. Which of your ideas did the class like best?

_____

_____

_____

Code!

Little Willy and Grandfather made up a code so that little Willy could understand Grandfather. If Grandfather put his hand palm down, it meant "no." Palm up meant "yes," one finger meant "I'm hungry," and two fingers meant "water."

You and your classmates will make a class code. First, write your own ideas for the code below. Then, share your ideas with the class. Together, everyone can choose the best ideas and make a class code chart. To help, your teacher can write the ideas on the chalkboard and the class can vote. "Speak" with this code as much as you can for **one week** in class!

MESSAGE	YOUR CODE
Yes.	_____
No.	_____
Thank you.	_____
Please.	_____
I'm thirsty.	_____
I'm hungry.	_____
I'm tired.	_____
I'm happy.	_____
I'm sad.	_____
Be quiet!	_____
May I sharpen my pencil?	_____
Open your book.	_____
Close your book.	_____
Your homework is. . .	_____
It's time to eat.	_____
It's time to exercise.	_____
It's time to go home.	

Think of one more message and the code for it.

Message: _____   Code: _____

Same and Different

Little Willy and Stone Fox are like each other in some ways. What are at least two ways they are the **same**?

1. _____

_____

_____

2. _____

_____

Can you think of another way they are the **same**?

_____

_____

Little Willy and Stone Fox are not like each other in some ways. What are at least two ways they are **different**?

1. _____

_____

_____

2. _____

_____

_____

Can you think of another way they are **different**?

_____

_____

_____

90

Good Reasons?

Both little Willy and Stone Fox wanted to win the race for good reasons.

What was the reason little Willy wanted to win? _____

_____

_____

Do you think his reason was a good one? _____

Why?_____

_____

_____

What was the reason Stone Fox wanted to win?

_____

_____

_____

Do you think his reason was a good one?

_____

Why?_____

_____

_____

Which reason do **you** think was better? _____

_____

Why?_____

_____

_____

_____

_____

_____

_____

Stone Fox and STONE FOX

If it is possible for you to see the made-for-television movie **Stone Fox*** after you have completed reading the book, do this activity.

List things that were the same in the book and the movie.

1. _____
2. _____
3. _____
4. _____
5. _____

List things that were different in the book and the movie.

1. _____
2. _____
3. _____
4. _____
5. _____

Which one did you like better? _____

Why?_____

_____

_____

*NBC, 1987

92

The Title Is. . .

The title of the book is **Stone Fox.** Do you like this title? _____

Why do you think the author, John Reynolds Gardiner, gave the book this title? _____

_____

_____

_____

_____

Write three new titles for the story that would give readers a good idea what the story is about.

1. _____

2. _____

3. _____

Which one of your titles do you like the best? _____

_____

Why?_____

_____

Do you like your title better than **Stone Fox?** _____

Why?_____

_____

_____

_____

Willy's Sled

MATERIALS: Scissors, glue, yarn, colored pencils, poster board, tape, two popsicle sticks.

DIRECTIONS:

1. Color Willy; cut around dotted and solid lines to make 2 halves at bottom.
2. Bend one half forward and one half towards the back.
3. Cut solid lines around sled; fold up on all dotted lines.
4. Curl long side around pencil to form front of sled.
5. Glue Tab A to Side A. Glue Tab B to Side B.
6. Glue Tabs C and D to Side C.
7. Glue a popsicle stick on each side of sled (see diagram).
8. Glue Willy's Tabs to inside of sled.
9. Punch a hole in Willy's hands.
10. Thread yarn through both hands; run up and over front of sled. Glue down.
11. Tape 2 sheets of poster board together; attach to wall to make a snow slide.
12. Have students estimate how many seconds it will take sled to go down the hill.

Activity: Estimated seconds _____

Actual seconds_____

TAB B

SIDE B

TAB C

SIDE C

TAB A

SIDE A

TAB D

About Love...

Stone Fox is a story about love. It is about the love a little boy has for his grandfather. It is about the love of a boy for his dog—and the love his dog has for him.

Complete these sentences about love:

1. Love is _____

   _____

   _____

   _____

   _____

2. I love _____

   _____

   _____

   _____

   _____

   _____

3. I show my love by _____

   _____

   _____

   _____

   _____

4. _____ (Write one or
   more names
   of people
   _____ you know
   who love
   _____ love(s) me! you.)

Responsible!

This story helps us learn about being responsible. Little Willy took the responsibility for taking care of his grandfather. He did things that many ten-year-olds could not or would not do to take care of his grandfather.

Read this definition of being responsible: Being responsible is being able to do a task or perform a duty by yourself. Being responsible means that someone can depend on you!

Using this definition, would you say that **you** are a responsible person?

☐ YES ☐ NO ☐ SOMETIMES

What is one thing that you are responsible for. . .

at home?_____

_____

at school? _____

_____

at play? _____

_____

Would you be able to be responsible for someone you love like little Willy was?_____ Why or how? _____

_____

_____

_____

96